4095

cool it
or
lose it !

BY *Dale Evans Rogers*

ANGEL UNAWARE
CHRISTMAS IS ALWAYS
DEAREST DEBBIE
MY SPIRITUAL DIARY
NO TWO WAYS ABOUT IT!
SALUTE TO SANDY
TIME OUT, LADIES!
TO MY SON
THE WOMAN AT THE WELL
DALE
COOL IT OR LOSE IT!

DALE EVANS ROGERS
RAPS WITH YOUTH

cool it
or
lose it!

FLEMING H. REVELL COMPANY
OLD TAPPAN, NEW JERSEY

Scripture references in this volume are from the *King James Version of the Bible.*

Excerpt from *Christ Is Alive* by Michel Quoist, translated by Jack F. Bernard. Copyright © 1971 by Doubleday & Company, Inc. Reprinted by permission of the publisher.

Library of Congress Cataloging in Publication Data

Rogers, Dale Evans.
   Cool it or lose it!

     SUMMARY: Discusses the importance of religion in daily life and how it can help young people deal with problems.
     1. Youth—Religious life. [1. Christian life]
I. Title.
BV4531.2.R585   248'.83   72-5348
ISBN 0-8007-0551-3

TO MY SON, Thomas Frederick Fox, whose steadfast Christian commitment throughout his life directly influenced my decision to commit my life to Jesus Christ. I am sure that many times during my turbulent years as an aspiring actress determined to succeed in show business, my son must have been tempted to lose his cool with his defiant floundering mother. He simply "kept on keeping on" as a Christian before me—until he won me to his Lord and Saviour.

TO THE COURAGE OF THE NOW GENERATION, whose dauntless search for truth is giving *my* generation pause for thought and self-examination.

TO THE COURAGE OF THE FLEMING H. REVELL COMPANY for publishing and retaining the title *Cool It or Lose It*, knowing that the title itself sounds controversial, and for their restraint in attempting to soften the tell-it-like-it-is quality of this writing which is meant to confront directly both generations with the dire need to negotiate meaningful communication of Christian concern.

Contents

Foreword

The written ministry of Dale Evans Rogers began with the publication of her first book, ANGEL UN-AWARE. Now, ten books later, she continues to reach more and more Americans of all ages.

Although her appeal is not limited to any one age group, Dale's particular feeling for, and sensitivity to young people has always shone through her writings. She and Roy shared their hearts and home with nine children. Their fourteen grandchildren are very much a part of their lives. In their constant travels throughout the country, Dale and Roy Rogers meet and talk to literally thousands of young men and women each year.

Roy and Dale are intimately concerned with the future of America and the young men and women who *are* its future. She asks some searching questions about our country and where it is going. What she has to say has special meaning not only for the young people with whom she is "rapping," but for all who care about America and its Christian destiny.

Fleming H. Revell Company is privileged to be a part of the ministry of Dale Evans Rogers.

THE PUBLISHERS

cool it
or
lose it !

1

Let's Rap....

Okay, let's rap!
In this book we're going to rap about parents who don't understand their children and children who don't understand their parents—about problems between the two that have us both uptight. Let's get two things straight about the two generations.

When I was a kid we spoke English—or, at least, we tried to. We had rules about our language, but that isn't necessarily so, today. A language that leaves me spinning every time I hear it is the lingo used by my children and grandchildren. It's enough to drive a conscientious teacher of English grammar stark, raving mad. We use the same words, but they don't mean the same thing.

A cat (when I was young) meant something that walked on four legs—now it means someone who walks on two legs. A chick was the son or daughter of a hen—now it's a girl. Bread was something to eat—now it's money. A pad was something you wrote on—now it's a place to live. A pot was something you put on the stove—now it's a weed you put in your mouth. A trip meant going to see Grandma at Christmas— now it means blowing your top.

And a rap was a blow, a sharp knock—today it is conversation, a discussion, or communication. I have a feeling that it may have come from the word *rapport*, but I may be wrong about that; maybe it's something you kids invented. Anyway, it is just another bit of evidence of the gap between your generation and mine.

The poor parents who read this book can either go out and buy a mod dictionary of the new lingo, or maybe, as we go along, you younger ones can interpret for them.

I am one of the over-thirties. I'd much rather be an under-thirty, but the calendar on my wall laughs out loud when I say that. I didn't have anything to say about this; like Topsy in *Uncle Tom's Cabin*, I just growed whether I liked it or not. I'm not ashamed of being over thirty; in some ways, I'm a lot happier than I was at thirteen. I learned a lot as I traveled the road you younger ones are traveling now, and the hard knocks I got on the trip taught me a lot that just might help you.

I can hear you saying, right now, "Huh! She's over thirty; that means she's Establishment, and we can't communicate with the Establishment." You think that rapping is impossible between us, but actually it isn't. You should know that when I was your age I thought the same thoughts about the older generation that you're thinking now. This Generation Gap business isn't anything new; it's old hat. There has *always* been a gap between generations and there *should* be. There's even a gap between those of you who are seventeen and those of you who are sneaking up on twenty. A college president said the other day that there was a wide gap between freshmen and sophomores!

Don't worry too much about it. The Gap will close. I am amazed today at the wisdom of my parents who I once thought were hopeless squares. It will happen to you, too.

Yes, I've been around for quite a spell. I had a good laugh, recently, as I sat waiting to be introduced as the speaker at a businessmen's luncheon—an Establishment affair. The chairman, whom I had never seen before, said, in presenting me, "I'm glad to meet you in person. For a long time I thought you were one of those show-business celebrities they fix up for the screen, and I doubted that you were the same sort of person in real life. But I must say that you bear inspection."

I didn't know whether to kiss him or kill him, but when I thought it over it made sense. It makes sense for a lot of us who are over thirty to inspect the opinions and ideas of those who are younger—meaning you!—and for those under thirty to inspect and respect the opinions and ideas of the oldsters before you start throwing rocks at them.

I know—when one passes thirty, that's it, man! They've had it. I thought I'd had it, too, on my thirtieth birthday. I was using a magnifying glass to find new lines on my face. The thought of a young crow's foot getting a toehold at the corners of the eyes made me think of Methuselah—or Methuselah's wife. Since prematurely gray hair is hereditary on one side of my family, I started tweezing out the gray ones at about the same time. But within a few years I gave up; I realized that aging is inevitable and that I might as well accept something I couldn't prevent anyway. Today, by the grace of God and with a little help now and then from Max Factor, I manage to look my best most of the time.

As a matter of fact, I get upset when I'm pressured to look like the teen-ager I just ain't, anymore. I refuse to wear mini-skirts; the sight of an adult woman wearing that getup in a pitiful attempt to look young makes me sick, and I'm all for you younger ones who resent their parents trying to be teen-agers in an attempt to communicate with them. It isn't for me!

We of the older generation are definitely *not* teen-agers. I heard a preacher recently offer another word for oldsters; he said we were *keen-agers*. Right on, preacher!

I'm not asking you to agree with him or with that definition, but I am asking you to give us an honest listen. Don't turn your backs on us because you think we are Establishment, and we've been around a little longer than you have.

First off, let's break down that word *establishment*. This word actually means, *fixed, sure.* What, in the light of technological advance, is *fixed* actually—for all time? In any area you care to mention, there is variance of opinion, and what seems fact today may be disproved tomorrow, next month, or next year. We are subject to change, and in the last fifty years, change has been constant. There is really only *One Establishment*—and GOD IS THE ESTABLISHMENT—for God is unchanging. The Bible says, ". . . with whom there is no variableness . . . of turning" (James 1:17)—and it also says, "Jesus Christ the same yesterday, and today and forever" (Hebrews 13: 8)—*Established*—He said, "I am the truth" (John 14: 6)! *Established.* He said, "I am the way." *Established.* He said, "I am the life." *Established.* We humans, the oldest and wisest of us—the most experienced of us— are fallible, prone to failure, change, decay.

Consider the position of science. There is absolutely nothing fixed in science, for we are ever learning. What seems fixed and absolute today may be completely obsolete next month or next year. GOD IS NEVER OBSOLETE; HE IS ESTABLISHED, IRRE-

VOCABLY, COMPLETELY CONTEMPORARY, REAL, AND RELATIVE TO EVERY GENER-ATION AND SEASON OF LIFE. As we give our-selves to God, through Jesus Christ, we are constantly, by Him and by His Holy Spirit, changed, molded, being conformed to the Image of Himself. In Him we live, move, and have our being. No, there is no real *Establishment*, save Almighty God, His Christ, His Holy Spirit—and in Him we become children of the King, established by Jesus Christ, through His Cross and Resurrection in our behalf. Don't call my genera-tion, or that before us, "Establishment"—and mean it, for the term is a misnomer. As a figure of speech, okay—just so we understand who the Real Establish-ment is!

Now, referring to so-called Establishment, you are a member of an establishment, too: You live in a society that is made up of a thousand "establish-ments." You can boast of being nonconformists, but from where I sit, you seem to be building a brand-new kind of conformity in which the boys wear long hair and straggly beards and ragged pants, and the girls wear maxicoats over hot pants and try to come to school in bare feet, as a sign that you are anti-Estab-lishment.

You young people have a point in challenging many of the values of my generation. True Americans and true Christians should examine themselves daily to see if they are "putting their money where their mouth is," but how many of *you* actually have the courage to be yourselves? Most of you, like most of us, are followers. If you are following a leader who bows not to God but only to himself, you are nowhere—you are lost—and so is that leader. If this is the case with you, or with the so-called Establishment, then both of you are slipping backwards. God is true advance, in any realm worth mentioning. Realize that we all are pilgrims, travelers on our earthly span of experience—that my generation has simply been on the road a little longer—that we are prone to failure, just as you are, and that we must both have compassion for the failure of each other. We must try to understand each other, and clasp hands, walking on by God's grace and training.

All right—if you can buy this—let's rap.

But let's make it an intelligent rap.

Let's keep it cool, lest we lose everything and gain nothing.

Let's admit that neither of us has all the answers nor the truth about everything all tied up in our own little bag. Okay?

2

Quite Out of Hand?

LET ME START by saying that I think you in the NOW generation are not as bad as you're cracked up to be. I read a little jingle the other day that went:

> This bearded youth, quite out of hand
> Is not exactly what we planned . . . .

But some of our planning wasn't so hot, either. A lot of you are rebelling against what Bishop Werner of the United Methodist Church calls "the unreality and dishonesty found in much of our society." I'm with you on that—at least on some of it.

John W. Rothney, in a magazine called *The Train Dispatcher*, says something about you and your revolt that sounds good to me:

Never have youth received as much criticism since the world began, but now we have more ways of doing it—television, the radio, more publication, etc. All this criticism of youth just isn't true. Kids these days are much better than we were as kids—they are better thinkers; they are better learners; they are much more democratic than you and I were and they are more self-disciplined.

On the whole, I agree. Many of you are bright and courageous and a lot more honest and forthright than were many of my generation. *And many of you are not.* There is a poisonous minority among you that is giving all of you a reputation you don't deserve. They are creating problems that don't exist by using violence as a means of answering very important problems. These could be settled with a little common sense and an appreciation of values—which we had better not lose if we want to survive!

You say you have problems that we never had? Maybe so—but we still had problems that looked pretty big, some of them still the same. When I was young, we had a problem with bootleg whiskey. We had problems with premarital and extramarital sex. We even had problems with jazz music and mod dances and skirts that right then were evolving into the modern mini-skirt. We had the same old racial discrimination and poverty—problems of disrespect— or with the idea that God was old-fashioned or even dead, or with appreciation of the truths and ideals of

the Bible. We honored our fathers and our mothers.
It was the rare child, not the usual one, who was
impudent to them.

Neither did our parents treat us like poor abused
little darlings when the teachers in school disciplined
us. They didn't rush off to berate the teacher; they
approved of what he had done. If we came home and
complained of correction in school, we got *another*
dose of correction from mother or dad. There was no
such thing as parents ganging up on a teacher to get
him fired. You had no business misbehaving in school;
you were there to obey and to learn, not to go out on
strike because you didn't like the janitor or because
the superintendent told you not to walk on the grass.
I may have an old-fashioned hang-up on this, but I
think the old saying is right: "To spare the rod is to
spoil the child."

We had prayer and short devotional services in my
high school. There was no compulsion about it; it was
something we did at home and in the church, and we
saw nothing wrong in doing it in school. We never
dreamed that one day an atheistic woman would make
a national problem of prayer in school, and start a
ruckus that would eventually outlaw prayer and the
Bible from the schoolroom.

There was a flag in the schoolroom, too. We meant
it when we pledged our devotion to it. We respected
the flag. We would have been pretty rough with any

boy or girl who dared insult it and all it stood for. I still respect that flag, and love it, and I do a burn that isn't slow when I see it torn up in the streets, spat upon, and even burned by wild-eyed fanatics who would be shot for doing it in Soviet Russia.

This is a nasty problem that we oldsters should have taken care of before it began to spread. Somewhere along the way we got fat and affluent and forgot the blessings we had received under that flag and took it all for granted and relaxed in our protection of its freedom. We slept while the enemies within became bolder and bolder—bold enough to wave a Viet Cong flag in their street demonstrations! We slept in heedlessness until now they make something more than a fair noise. They would con you of the NOW generation into rejecting the American way of life. They are brutally wrong; they would have you help them in destroying the basic American principle—the pursuit of life, liberty, and happiness.

There is a fine Jewish rabbi down in Miami who says it for me:

The violence of such protestors brings out, very often, the worst moods and traits of those defending the law of the land. In plain words, violence begets violence. Jeers and sneers and taunts turn into brick-throwing; warnings turn into tear gas; injury turns into wounds and wounds turn to killings and death. For all these reasons, I for one believe it is a mistake for dissidents to unite in these mass demonstrations. In this kind of alliance, a few sick individuals can transform a gathering into a mob. And the action of such a mob, using obscene language on banners, burning draft cards and trampling on the flag, will evoke, rightly I think, the worst fears, prejudices and reactions from the nation as a whole.

I do not ask you to wave the American flag wherever you go, actually or metaphorically. I know very well that flag-wavers can be un-American in their every word and deed. True patriotism involves more than saluting the flag and pledging obedience. Nevertheless I think you must honor the flag for the good it represents. America is still a free nation—freer than any other in the world. America did help destroy the Nazi tyranny in Europe. It has given untold fortunes to the poor and underprivileged nations of the world, risking even their enmity in spite of that aid. And countless numbers of Americans, from Jefferson to Lincoln to Roosevelt and Kennedy, have inspired freedom-loving people everywhere.

For these reasons, and for many reasons not given here, the American flag should be honored, present feelings of protest notwithstanding. In any event, it must not be burned. Flag-burning is an act of desperation that can only call forth desperate acts from others. And it misses the mark entirely. We do not burn the Bible because some people kill and steal. Yet the Bible is the printed symbol of the values, ideals and goals we cherish.

Flag-honoring, yes! Flag-waving, maybe! Flag-burning, NO!

JOSEPH R. NAROT
*Letters to the NOW
Generation*

Let's get another thing straight about all this—these insults to the flag, our downgrading of respect for the Constitution, our abuses of our spiritually-inspired laws *in no way diminish these essential values.* Some of you have not been told enough of the spiritual influences behind the values—and my generation must take most of the blame for that. And if we and you together go on allowing the enemies of these sacred values to have their way—if you and your children lose this precious heritage of freedom under law and under God—we will only have ourselves to blame.

Cool it, youth—or lose it!

The father of Stuart Hamblen (lay preacher and

writer of country, western and gospel songs) put it on the line when he said, "If some of these people who scream for their constitutional rights got them, they would be hanged for treason." Treason is the betrayal of one's country—and when these people march in our streets under the flag of the Viet Cong they betray their country, and they could be hanged for that! It seemed for a while that this word *treason* was becoming irrelevant and obsolete, but today many of us are taking a second look at the word, and are beginning to speak out about it. Mothers and fathers who have lost sons in two world wars and in various other wars are beginning to resent the sneers leveled at their sons and brothers and husbands, who fought in good faith that they were there to protect this priceless freedom for all the world. They are getting hot under the collar at the shameful turncoating of the draft-dodgers in this land of the free and this home of the brave—a land made free and kept free by those who did *not* turn their coats, but died in them in the blessed hope that their sons and brothers and husbands wouldn't have to die. I, for one, take a very dim view of this turncoat treason, whether it comes in a boy who accepts the dearly-bought freedom handed down to him by an American soldier who gave his life for it and refuses to offer any sacrifice whatever on his part, or in the turncoat radical who sends his followers out to die in a riot and then runs to Algeria when the going gets rough. We all love a hero—but what's heroic about a coward in hiding?

Kick that one around a while!

And this—suppose these traitors win, suppose they destroy flag, constitution, values, and all—*what do you have left? Where do you go from there?*

3

Don't Be Used!

FREEDOM is the most overworked word in our modern vocabulary—and it seems to mean different things to different people. When, for instance, I see a TV shot of students rioting against ROTC, I wonder if the rioters want freedom or just want their own way. Nobody is forcing them to join ROTC; you don't have to join it if you don't want to—but what right do the violent ones have to deny another student the right to join, if he wants to? What kind of freedom is *that?*

And I see something else, here. I see fewer and fewer students throwing the rocks. A lot of these fellows don't look much like students to me; they are not young; they are hardened professionals who will never see thirty again. Look closely, and you'll find these old pros whipping it up from Berkeley to Columbia.

Do you know who they are? They've told us, in plain language. They are men who would destroy our national defense system as a first step toward abolishing the American government. Don't take my word for it—read what they say. They even led a mob in Washington with the avowed purpose of "stopping the government"—blocking entrances to the administration buildings so that the administrative machinery couldn't function. It was a stupid idea, impossible of realization; it was a flop, and fortunately for all of us it didn't come off. True, there wasn't much actual violence in that affair, but the *purpose* of the whole plot was violent in concept. Someone planted bombs in the Capitol building before the marchers arrived. That was violent. It was also treason. And it was no accident—it was planned!

There's too much of a plan involved in all this. It is planned not so much by young college students as it is by seasoned pros who don't care a fig about your freedom, who would destroy your future by poisoning your minds, your bodies, and your spirits with drugs, pornography, free-wheeling sex, and flowing promises of a new order of peace in which everybody will love his brother because "the evils of imperialism and capitalism will be destroyed." They hold up the sign of peace with one hand and throw a bomb with the other. What kind of peace is that—and what kind of "new order" do you think we'll get if they get control?

Don't buy it, youth! *They are using you.* They are deceiving you into destroying the government—and when you lose they'll skedaddle for Algiers and leave you holding the bag.

Maybe you'll remember the riot that broke out in Pittsburgh, the year the Pittsburgh Pirates won the World Series. They had a celebration in Pittsburgh, and usually there isn't anything wrong with a celebration. But this one turned out to be one of the most disgusting riots in the city's history. The crowds in the streets went crazy; cars were overturned, and some cars were set afire. There was bitter fighting between the police and the rioters, and a lot of people were hurt. It didn't just *happen*—this brawl was planned by a bunch of hard-core radicals who capitalized on the excitement among perfectly innocent sport enthusiasts, and all of a sudden—pow!

This is when the radical strikes and gets in his dirty work; that's when the knives and the rocks and the guns come out. They *use* people who would never be a part of such a rotten business under ordinary circumstances. Anything can happen when the devil gets a grip on us when we're emotionally overwrought. I'll wager that most of that Pittsburgh crowd didn't know what they were doing—didn't know they were being *used*.

A few years back President Nixon was traveling across the country in a political campaign. His helicopter landed at Ocean Grove, New Jersey. There was the usual handful of protestors in the crowd who did some shouting of words that cannot be printed here, but nobody threw any rocks or bottles. One of the President's party said to a bystander, "I can't believe it! This is the only place in the United States where we have landed without being stoned!"

Now it is a pretty sad state of affairs when an American president is treated like that. There was a time when we respected the presidential office, or at least gave the president a chance to speak his piece, whether we agreed with him or not. Apparently that's out now, for some Americans.

There were only a few young college students in that Ocean Grove crowd, and they did *not* do any yelling or obscene protesting. What little disturbance there was, was raised by the same old professionals whose business is violence. That encourages me; it's a good sign, and it seems to be happening more and more. College deans and presidents are telling us that many of the students, realizing that their violence has done their cause more harm than good, have turned back to their books and to another more powerful and influential form of protest—that of Jesus Christ! It's a startling development, and it is spreading fast. It is breaking down a lot of the old denominational barriers; it is known popularly as the Jesus Movement, and a Catholic leader in California says of it, "We are on the threshold of the greatest spiritual revival the United States has ever experienced."

It is reaching out far beyond the college campus.

Thousands of them are found in the ranks of the Jesus People, who are also known as Street Christians or Jesus Freaks; they have six hundred centers across the country. The Catholic Pentecostals have been called "the most dramatic movement in modern Catholicism," it goes upwards of ten thousand members. All over the country there are hundreds of thousands involved in a huge youth revival. Big names are among them—singers Johnny Cash and Eric Clapton; Paul Stookey of Peter, Paul, and Mary has preached on the steps of Berkeley's Sproul Hall; Pat Boone played the lead in the movie version of *The Cross and the Switchblade* and has baptized (to date) more than two hundred converts in his own swimming pool.

I saw something the other day that really made me cheer. I happened to pass Ciro's famous restaurant in Hollywood, and I looked 'way back in my life to the day when I was taken there for dinner, during my first tests for the movies. It was a fancy den, in those days, but today, lo and behold, it is a Jesus People coffee house. On the door is a huge picture of Jesus with the caption JESUS, THE LIBERATOR! You may call that happenstance; I call it a miracle. It made me think of Billy Graham's estimate of the Jesus People: "If this is a fad, I welcome it." No fad!

4

Revelation at Costa Mesa

I REALLY GOT INSIDE this Jesus Movement one Sunday evening not long ago; my two granddaughters, who are college students at Biola (The Bible Institute of Los Angeles), took me by the hand and led me to a Jesus People meeting. "Grandma Dale, you'll *love* it." I wasn't so sure, but when you get orders from your grandchildren, you go! They went regularly every Sunday evening for intensive Bible study. We arrived an hour ahead of time, and it's a good thing we did, for most of the seats in the chapel were already filled. There were people of every human variety: young ones with long hair, young and old ones with beards, some barefoot, some in patchjeans, some clean-shaven and well dressed; they were middle-aged, young and old, some young people with babies in their arms—a real cross section of our society. I was deeply impressed by their numbers and their enthusiasm, but I couldn't help wondering, at first, just what was going to happen. All of them had one thing in common. They all brought their Bibles.

It was a very warm night, and that added to the early confusion. By seven o'clock they were sitting in the aisles, on the floor near the minister, and all over the platform. A lot more were standing outside, near the doors and open windows—and they stood there for two-and-a-half hours. We sang the choruses of old and new gospel hymns without any accompaniment, and they *knew* those songs by heart. At one point we were told to put our arms around the persons next to us, and the rows of people swayed gently to the joyous rhythm. It was all done reverently and in perfect order—a delightful and refreshing combination.

After the song service (why have so many churches dropped this singing service in their worship?) everyone opened his Bible and listened intently for two hours as the minister led in the study of several New Testament chapters—*chapters*, not verses taken out of context. There was not a sound in the room, except for his voice—no rustling, no restlessness, no whispering, no boredom—just a deep interest and hunger for plain down-to-earth teachings of the Gospel of Jesus Christ. You could have heard the proverbial pin drop—it was so quiet.

When the minister had finished, a lovely young girl sang a few of her own original songs of testimony as she strummed her guitar, in a hauntingly beautiful voice. As she sang, I heard the bells of heaven ring.

There were prayers that sank deep into the heart, and then they filed out quietly into the night. There was none of that after-the-service gossip that destroys the wholesome effects of worship in so many of our churches.

To me, it was a revelation. At times, I looked at them almost in amazement; you don't see this sort of thing very often! Here was a group of people from every condition of life, from every denomination in Protestantism (plus many who were affiliated with no church at all) who were utterly sincere in concentrating on how to live the Way, the Truth, and the Life—which means knowing Jesus Christ. It was my first participation in Christian worship with a large number of Jesus People, and it will not be my last. I came away from that church with a new song in my heart for the future, and with a new confidence in our young people.

God has always had enough of His people—people such as the dedicated minister at Calvary Chapel, and the lay leaders of this congregation—to spread the gospel and to stand for complete commitment to Christ, regardless of the depravity and decadence of the world. The youth of today live surrounded by temptations that we never knew when we were young; many of them are the victims of overpermissive parents who close their eyes to the dangers involved in these temptations. There are those in the estab-

lished church who disapprove of the dress and the
haircuts and the religious performances of many of
the Jesus People who, frankly, are a bit far-out. How-
ever, they cannot in conscience doubt the sincerity
in their quest to know and to offer a new attitude to
their Lord. I'm for them; I'm for any man, woman or
child who is sincerely reaching for the hand of Jesus
Christ, and these people are reaching. I say, Lord,
bless them, teach them, and mold them in your image.
My Bible says, " . . . [My word] shall not return unto
me void . . . " (Isaiah 55:11). When that Word is
warmly planted in the heart, it just *has* to bear fruit!
God does not promise and then fail to deliver.

People often ask me what these Jesus People mean
to the future of the church—and whether the church
should take them in, even when they are so often a
so-called disturbing element with their new, odd ways
of worship, and their (often) somewhat weird con-
ceptions of what religion is all about. I think the
churches—all the churches—should welcome them.
These kids are the church of tomorrow; before we
know it, they will be running things both within and
without the church. I feel that even though local
churches may not agree with their forms of worship
they should invite them in. (Jesus, you know, spent
much of His time with those who did not believe at
all, and talked with many different types of people.)
I think the church should listen to them and to their

witness. I think that some of what is really good in them might rub off on the church and supply a warmth that is missing among so many of us oldsters in the pews who don't want to change *anything*. The church should adopt whatever is good in them—good such as I saw that night in the little chapel in Costa Mesa. I think that both we and they can learn much from the other. To shut the door against them would be to do something that the Master would *never* do.

5

Music That Rocks the Soul

A LOT OF MY FRIENDS are disturbed by what they call the crazy music of some of the Jesus People. They call it rock 'n' roll, but it really isn't—at least it isn't the shoutin'-and-screamin' stuff that some identify with the hippies. If I don't lose too many friends in saying it, let me say that I don't know of any reason why we should oppose any religious music simply because it's new or different. You know, John and Charles Wesley, who were the early leaders of the Methodist Church in England, were severely criticized when they wrote some new hymns that were different from those that had been sung for generations in the established Church of England. The old hymns and rituals were good, and the people loved them, but the Wesleys were on fire with a blazing evangelism that called for something livelier and more inspiring to the sinners in the streets. Many in the church thought the Wesley gospel songs were just plain awful—irreverent, imbecilic, gross, slangy, fantastic, cheap, undignified, offensive and a lot more! (Imagine calling "Come, thou al-

mighty king" or "Hark, the herald angels sing" undignified or offensive!) But we still sing the Wesley
hymns—especially their *gospel* hymns—and we love
them because they are pure gospel and they spell out
salvation in terms we understand. Innovations are
nothing new; every translation of the Bible was, in
its time, an innovation!

I don't quarrel with this new music of youth; I
welcome it, and I have used quite a bit of it in our
shows and public appearances, mixing it up with the
older gospel tunes. Just a little while ago I made an
album of a number of songs that I wanted to call *On
the Rock*.

I wanted to call it that because one of my favorite
hymns is "Rock of Ages," a song that has a very
special meaning for me. Shortly after Roy and I were
married, our minister, Dr. Jack MacArthur, preached
a sermon on "The Home That Is Built on the Rock."
I didn't want our new home to blow away in a storm;
I wanted it grounded on the Rock of Ages. So not
long ago, when my new record album was in prepara-
tion, that sermon popped up in my mind, and we
tentatively decided to feature the term "rock" in the
title. To this album we added two other favorites,
"The Old Rugged Cross" and "In the Garden," which
happened to be the first song I ever sang in public (in
church when I was nine years old).

The album is now on the stands under the title

Faith, Hope and Charity. The recording company had second thoughts about a title with "rock" in it because of objection to rock gospel music in some quarters of the church. They also wanted to use the title *Faith, Hope and Charity* since many people will recognize the phrase from my own composition, "The Bible Tells Me So," which is also included in the album. I understand their reasoning about changing the title, though I am sorry they felt it necessary due to some people's prejudice about rocka-my-soul type of gospel music. I also sang one of the gospel songs the kids of today are singing, "Stranger of Galilee," as well as "Pass It On" and "Lord, to My Heart Bring Back the Spring Time." The old and the new—and all pure gospel.

Everywhere we go today, I sing one that has caught the imagination of youth—"Put Your Hand in the Hand of the Man Who Stills the Waters." That, my friend, is a *great* song! The kids love it, and it rocks my soul to hear them sing it. It's a hit with them—thank God—because it tells the gospel truth they long to hear. They have learned the truth that He *did* still the waters, that He *did* calm the sea, that He *has* conquered the tempests in their hearts. They've tried just about everything else, and it hasn't worked. Christ *has* worked in them; they are working to make this Christ real to others who like themselves have known sin and error, and they love those others. That is Christian conviction. That is awareness of His truth—and if the awareness came out of that song, then I will sing it with them until I die!

To my generation, I say: Don't laugh at their music, study it! analyze it! It may be different in beat or rhythm, but it is a song of salvation sung in the wilderness of their world.

May I make a suggestion—or rather mention what some of our churches are doing about all this? Many of the older folks like the older forms of worship, and the old songs of the faith, sung to the accompaniment of the church organ. They should not be deprived of that; all of us should be free to worship God as we please. But many churches have found a good answer to the problem. Their morning worship is formal, in the old order, and the hymns they sing are the tried and true old hymns, but at night they turn the worship service over to the young people, allowing them to sing their new, contemporary songs, and to study the Scriptures and give their testimonies in their own lingo. They tell the youth to organize their own groups for Bible reading and discussion, and I think that is wonderful and healthy. I have a feeling that as these younger ones mature and grow older, they will develop a modified form of worship. I think that *is* happening, already, as I saw it happen in the Costa Mesa chapel.

After all, what's wrong with raising your hands as well as your voices, to praise the Lord?

6

A Real Revolutionary

LET'S LOOK AT ANOTHER ANGLE. Every now and then I meet some lovable young rebel who says to me, when I question some of his revolutionary tactics, "Well, Jesus was revolutionary, wasn't He?" He sure was—with a difference. He was revolutionary in His *thinking*. He said, " ... I am not come to destroy, but to fulfil" (Matthew 5:17). He also cautioned us to obey those in authority, and to "Render ... unto Caesar the things which are Caesar's; and unto God the things that are God's." (22:21). He never advocated violence; many overenthusiastic fanatics and zealots would have welcomed Him as leader of a violent revolution against Rome—but this He would not do. He knew that the penalty of life without rules and government was chaos.

He was revolutionary in condemning the tyranny of undisciplined self and selfishness. He detested deceit and dishonesty in word, thought, and deed. But with His complete honesty and His unfeigned love for all people, He helped the afflicted and the downtrodden.

He forgave the trespasser, He raised the standards of men's lives. Like a whip He cut through pride and prejudice. He fearlessly told it like it was when He saw greed and hypocrisy. For such revolutionary thinking and for His declaration of His Sonship with God, He was nailed to a cross. He promised His followers that they, too, would be crucified, if they thought as He did. The way of the revolutionist is hard.

Put this in your notebook: *Jesus didn't tear down the Temple; He cleansed it.*

Young people, why aren't you more interested in cleansing than in destroying? Why don't you get about your Father's business of restoration? To set a fire, to detonate a bomb, to deface a flag requires no genius. But to build the fires of hope—Ah! there is achievement!

Why don't you try to prove our laws before trying to disprove them? The way to prove them is to test them. Abide by them. Set an example for us old Established hypocrites. Change us!

Lead us—but make no mistake about it—*you cannot lead us unless God leads you.* With Him, minorities of the most unlikely people down through the centuries have been the leavening, cleansing agents in human society. Because of His power in their yielded lives, many abuses and social sicknesses have been abolished, and He can do the same thing through you—you who are our NOW—if you will stand and be counted for Him.

There was plenty of corruption in the governments of Jesus' day, but He never said, "Destroy the government." There is plenty of corruption in the governments of our time, but to destroy them would only increase the corruption in another direction. You don't kill the dog to get rid of a few fleas!

Let's not forget that we the people are the government. We elect those who govern us, and it is just possible that a lot of the corruption gets started with us in the voting booth, electing men not fit to hold office. We can start cleaning *there*. Abolishing government after it is elected is no answer! Abolish it, and you still haven't solved the age-old problem of inherent evil lurking in every human heart. Only the penetrating searchlight of the Holy Spirit, of the Living God, can sweep out lust, greed, lying, stealing, and in their places put faith, hope, and charity.

We can take all the vast accumulated wealth of these United States, divide it equally, give everyone the same amount of land, and a good house, eliminate God and the so-called capitalistic system, and watch what happens. You'll see the same old conniving and undercover trading for advantage being reborn, and all the old prejudices starting all over again.

First, the heart must be changed. After that, the real, constructive revolution begins!

Watch it, youth. Don't be sold a phoney bill of goods by those who would exploit you for a godless system that has never worked and never will work. Take a good honest look at those countries in which God is denied. Rap a little with some of the refugees from the iron-curtain countries, and they will describe what life in hell is really like! They wouldn't have anything to gain in lying about conditions of life over there; they know a lot more about it than one who has never been there, and has no intention of going there! Listen to them. Ask them what happens to the man who shoots a cop in those countries. Take a long look at these people who are ready to risk their lives to come to the United States in an effort to get a breath of the blessed fresh air of freedom—and ask yourself if you would like to be one of them.

I am privileged to share in the ministry of a remarkable present-day missionary to (of all places!) the United States. His name is Ben Song, and he is from Seoul, Korea, birthplace of our Debbie Lee (In Ai Lee). This dedicated man of God lived through one revolution and he is now seeing first-hand in our own country what some are calling revolution. Ben Song is grateful to the United States for helping his homeland. His gratitude toward our country is not shared by those who forget—if they ever knew—the origin of our laws, courts, and just why you should respect them. The men who framed our constitution were men who believed in freedom and dignity for the individual under God.

Do you really want any other kind of freedom? Or do you want a dictatorship which would make *your* ideas of freedom obligatory for everybody?

Give me your answer to that question—and make it honest!

7

Your Pick of Pollutants

Up to now, we've been concentrating on talking about war and riots and protests and patriotism—because I think these may be the high-priority problems of American youth. But there are other problems. Let's get on to them.

Do you honestly want free sex, as so many of you say you do? Do you really, in your hearts, want to abolish marriage? Do you honestly think it is impossible to love the girl you marry so much that you don't *want* to cheat on the side? (Man, there are animals who are smarter that that; some animals actually practice monogamy!)

At the Manson murder trial, one of the woman defendants said that her little girl could be the daughter of any one of three men—she didn't know which. She may be free to live that way if she wants to, but how free is the baby who must live out her life under the shadow of illegitimacy? Would you choose such a way to come into the world?

(I also read what Charles Manson's mother said of him, when he was a young growing boy—"If Charles wanted anything, I'd give it to him." *Anything?* Well, it figures!)

If you'll forgive the crudity of an old countryism that I heard as a child: "A pig wouldn't eat *that* slop!"

A teen-ager named Mike Cope is quoted in *Christian Youth Today* as saying "This generation has been spoiled rotten. Parents have given kids so much in order to buy their love and respect that they've blown everything. But what's really bad is that the parents don't even realize that there is a Generation Gap. The bridge between them can only be built with a love that isn't bought." Right on, Mike!

Cool it! Think it over carefully before you decide how you're going to live—which values you will live by. Right now you are being encouraged, as Charles Manson was, to do your thing—*anything*—wherever and whenever you want to do it, and never mind the consequences. Hooray for lust! After all, you can take the pill or have an abortion, no matter what the side effects may be. Live it up, for tomorrow you may die. You call that being *free*?

I call it pollution.

Yes, we're all steamed up about air and water pollution. How about soul pollution? Both generations are involved in this pollution, whether we admit it or not. It's the fault of all of us, and we will have to work out the solution together. It didn't get this way in a day or a year, and it won't be conquered in a day or a year, but, with God's help, we can lick it!

I think we can use the church as a headquarters in attacking this problem. That's why I go up and down the country asking youth to stay in the church and stay in the church school, and in the youth fellowships of the church. There are people there who will help you hold that line.

Study your Bibles in church and church school, and your American history, and see how closely connected they are. It will be a long study, and it will not be easy, but in the end it will be worth all the blood, sweat, and tears that it takes. It will give you a strong rock to stand on. It will give you the very strength of Jesus Christ!

I was giving my testimony in a Texas city, not long ago, at a city-wide revival meeting. At one of the meetings, a fine young man who had been the leader of a gang of hoodlums called the Banditos, found Christ in a very real, personal, and life-changing encounter. That was good for him but it spelled danger for him at the hands of the gang. They threatened his life; they told him that nobody—but nobody—ever left that gang. The word was out that if he ever dared show himself in their territory again he'd be wiped out.

He went right into their territory and told *them* something, "You can kill me if you want to, but give me this one break—don't kill me until you've attended a revival meeting with me." For some reason known only to God, they accepted the proposal; eighteen of them came to the meeting, heard what was said, and accepted it. The boy is still alive and working among them, winning more.

That's what I mean by getting the very strength of Jesus Christ.

8

Let's Hear It for Discipline

Roy has just told me that he thinks I was a little rough and maybe a little unfair in telling that story about Mike Cope, and parents spoiling their children. He may have something there. *All* parents aren't spoiling their kids rotten, but I still think that we parents (that includes *me*) should be helping our kids in ways that we have neglected too much.

One is to understand that our children need models more than critics, in their parents. Another is to go all out in the effort to convince our children that there is an Unseen Member of the family who is always present in the house. We should be firm but loving in the discipline of the child, and we would be smart to start disciplining them by disciplining ourselves—showing them by example that discipline is vital to the molding of a good life. Let's be willing to laugh at *ourselves*, now and then, and teach them that there are times when they should laugh at *themselves*. Let's take God seriously, but not ourselves. Let's be willing to laugh together, cry together, work together, play together, worship together. Let's bridge the gap between us with Jesus Christ—who bridged the greater gap between man and God. He is our hope. It is His discipline of love that truly shapes our ends and makes our character.

When our little Debbie was killed in a bus accident, our son Dusty (Roy, Jr.) said to me, "Mom, we'd better start believing in Jesus Christ, right now." Right now! He probably didn't know it but he was echoing the words of St. Augustine: "Our hearts are restless until we find our rest in Thee." Amen!

Again, we should understand that the wise child respects and even *wants* discipline.

And last but not least, we should *not* "give them everything they want because when we were kids we didn't get everything *we* wanted." Let me illustrate this.

When we were working day and night on our TV series, we had to have someone in the house to take care of the children, and we found a sweet and wonderful lady who seemed perfect for that difficult job. She was gentle and kind, modest and retiring and soft-spoken, and not a strong-armer, if you know what I mean. But she had trouble, at first, with young Dusty who eyed her as an intruder. She wasn't *his* mother, so why should she be there at all? He tried to ignore her in his teen-age aloofness, and after that had gone on for some time, she said to him, "Dusty, I don't think you like me. I've tried to be good to you, like a good friend, but you don't seem to want that. Tell me—what is it about me that you don't like?"

And Dusty said, "Well, you don't holler at me!"

So—even though it went against her grain—she hollered at him—and *then* he thought she was great! After that—no trouble.

I think young people—especially very young people—get the idea that if you don't correct them and give them ground rules for their behavior, that you don't care about them. They think you're just too busy, or that you are *afraid* to "let them have it."

And when we go to the other extreme and give them too much, when we buy anything they think they want, we are as wrong as we would be if we gave them nothing. It isn't their fault that they have too much; it's our fault.

In our home, we used to tell the gang about how hard we had it when we were young, about that awful depression when we hardly had enough to eat, let alone getting a pile of presents at Christmas as high as the Empire State Building. That didn't get to them, at all; they would pull that old stunt of playing an imaginary violin, grinning like Cheshire cats. We would tell them, for instance, about how tough Roy had it when he was their age, living on a hardscrabble farm with his father working in a shoe factory to make ends meet. Roy was plowing on that farm when he was seven years old; he says there were more stumps on that farm than there was good soil! At Christmastime he would get some fruits and nuts and maybe even a little candy—and a new pocketknife. If it was a good year, they might have chicken for Christmas dinner, but that was about it. One Christmas Day he lost his new knife, and he cried all day, and the next day his dad—who couldn't bear to see him cry—went to town and bought him another knife. Roy loved his dad for that—the father had sacrificed for his son!

No wonder Roy got upset—and often a little angry—when *his* children got mountains of presents, ripped off the wrappings, one after another, and threw them aside to open the *next* one! They treated the deluge of presents as something they were entitled to, and when all the packages were opened they more than once looked around as if to say, "Is that *all?*" Before the day was over they were cutting up the cartons and the boxes (with my precious kitchen knives!) and playing with them instead of with the toys. Roy would almost have a fit; he'd say, "Next Christmas, all you're going to get is a bunch of empty boxes and a knife," and he'd go into the old routine about the little pocketknife his father had given him, and how he appreciated it as though it were made of pure gold—and then one of them would smile and start playing that imaginary fiddle.

It didn't help much when I tried to tell them about the sad Christmases *I* had during the depression, when, to feed my son Tom and myself, I would make a meal out of a pork chop bone and an onion, and give him a piece of bread off my plate that I should have eaten myself. (I wound up with a severe case of anemia, thanks to that near-starvation diet.) But that didn't get through to them, either. For, you see, they never had been through a depression; they didn't know what the word meant. They had always had enough to eat, always enough toys, always enough clothes.

We had to put a stop to it, and we did. We stopped splurging. I saw to it that they were never better dressed than the other children in their school. I made them understand the value of money—that it didn't grow on trees, and that because they were the children of successful Roy Rogers they would not be permitted to have all the money they wanted and spend it like young spendthrifts. When we took them along to perform in our shows, I insisted that they be paid the regular salaries on the scale set by the American Guild of Variety Artists—and I also insisted that they put what they earned in the bank. By the time they were in their teens, they had a nice little nest egg. The moment they were sixteen, the children took the course in Driver's Education and bought cars *with their own money.* We wouldn't let them buy new cars; they had to be secondhand—which they could afford without going broke.

Dusty bought himself an old '47 Chevy, and he and his pals had the time of their lives stripping it down and making it look like a cross between a stage coach and a miniature railroad locomotive. They made the back high and the front low so they could get away fast—you know, burn the rubber. He paid for the whole thing with his own money. He drove it to school when he had it "all set" (proud as Punch), only to park it beside a brand-new Thunderbird driven by one of those sharp-dressed kids who looked at Dusty's rattletrap Chevy as though it was something out of the Ark. He said to Dusty, "What are you driving that junk for? Your dad is Roy Rogers, and you're driving *that?* My father is just a screenwriter, and look what I'm driving!"

And good old Dusty said to him, "Well, did you buy it with your own money, or your dad's? I worked and paid for this Chevy, and it's *mine.*" I was never so proud of him as when he said that.

What I'm saying is that when we load our children down with luxuries we're not doing them any favors; when we make them work for it they will have a sense of pride and responsibility for something they have *earned.* And a sense of self-respect.

The same thing holds across the whole area of permissiveness—I mean those areas in which the child is not restricted in *anything*. No restrictions means no respect—for themselves or their parents. The parent doesn't get that respect by playing year-round Santa Claus.

So I say to all parents, present and future, let's quit turning children into selfish little ingrates. And while we're at it, let's get it straight that while it is good to be a pal to your child, it's a lot more important to be a parent!

9

Hey, Mom! Are You Listening?

IF I COULD RAP with your mothers for awhile, I'd have a few reminders for them.

Roy has a popular record of a country song entitled "Money Can't Buy Love." Aside from his fine job of singing it, the song says a mouthful—a heartful. Money has never bought love between lovers or between parents and children. A five-dollar bill is a poor substitute for love and interest in a child. A fiver is soon spent, leaving the child still hungry for the satisfaction and security of knowing that his parents really care enough about him to get deeply involved with him.

My generation, in the wake of two world wars, has been guilty of not getting involved—enough. Many mothers had to work during wartime, and all too often they came home to a hungry daddy and children who needed them, and they refused to act like mothers and keepers of the home fires. They preferred to work for the extra car, TV, or mink coat, and by the time night came they'd had it, and they didn't have much left for the family. Many a child grew up against a background of no cookies and milk after school, skimpy dinners, and no real companionship with mother and father. We got a rebellious generation out of that—which was just what we deserved!

The younger mothers of today don't remember those war years, and many of them are demanding what their working mothers had demanded—earlier— "We want to be liberated!" Liberated from what? From the privilege of motherhood—the greatest gift God could give them? Do they want their children to grow up in frustration and rebellion, seeking in destructive ways for that which should have been given them by their mothers?

I read a magazine article about "The Myth of Motherhood." What do you mean, myth? Those of you who have enjoyed the divine benediction of holding your baby in your arms for the first time know the unspeakable happiness of that moment—and it's no myth! Its blessing is very, very real.

Yes, I know there is a population explosion. God knows it, too. But if planned parenthood should become binding law, you childless parents would still have the option of adopting a homeless child and thus fulfill your mother-longing. Yes, I know there is a movement, calling for twenty-four hour nurseries that would supposedly free the mother. I suppose, in some instances, such a non-mother nursery might be good, but I also know that when you rob a child of tender loving care as an infant, that child, as an adult, is seldom able to either accept or give love to anyone else.

The hand that rocks the cradle can either wreck or rule the world. Are we bent on wrecking it, after all this time and experience? Of course childbearing and child rearing is often hard, monotonous, and thankless. What isn't? I have worked as a career woman in the business world and in "show biz," and I can tell you that it became dreary and monotonous and almost unbearable, at times. You work a lifetime at a desk and then you retire—to what? To unbearable loneliness?

There are some women who are especially gifted for service in other areas than motherhood, and some may be happier working in those other areas, but by and large I have found the happiest women functioning in the role of mothers. Some women are forced to work, and they need the help of nurseries, but certainly no child should be left in an impersonal children's institution an hour longer than necessary. I am not interested, here, in arguing the pros and cons of Women's Lib, nor in debating their principles—some of which are good (the earlier Lib movement which gave women the vote was *very* good). I appreciate all that, but I am still convinced that there is something even more important than the right to vote, or the right to equal work for equal pay. I am pleading for an increased effort to hold our homes together for the sake of the little people. Who, in a county or state or local nursery, will take time out to say to a frightened child, "God loves you; you do not need to be afraid"?

My attitude comes out of personal experience. Being in the entertainment business for most of our lives, Roy and I were away from home much of the time—too much of the time. Our children were deprived of our attention—the older ones, most of all. By the time I was able to devote more time to our home and to the children, my son Tom and the three older girls were married. I realized then that it was not a good arrangement working twelve to fourteen hours a day on a TV series and coming home at night exhausted, and trying to be a helpful and understanding mother in the few hours I had with them. I tried and tried hard, but it just didn't work. It was wrong, and I deeply regret it.

Working with my husband in show biz was, in a way, insurance against the misunderstandings that come so often with the separation of man and wife working on separate locations—the husband in Hollywood and the wife in New York! and so often ending in divorce. Working side by side was good, but I still feel that our children suffered during the day, even though we had the help of some wonderful, dedicated people substituting for us in our home. When at last I could stay home, I found the four younger children to be quite a handful, but I pitched in gung-ho and did my best with them. Many the time I wondered whether they or I would survive the struggle! Somehow, we did; we made up for a lot of lost time, and those were the happiest years of my life.

Our house is all too quiet now. How I long to hear, "Hey, Mom, what's for dinner?" Yes, I cooked the dinners then, did my own housework and shopping, even did our own laundry, and I'm glad I did—Women's Lib to the contrary. I desperately needed to do my thing as wife and mother, and I found a joy beyond reckoning in being just a plain, ordinary, everyday housewife. I still enjoy working with Roy in our personal appearances, but the personal appearances I enjoy most are those I have in our Christian home and those in which I stand before an audience and tell them what God has done for me and for us, and what He can do for them. For God has shown me that a Christian woman is happiest when she is managing things as a Christian woman, in the home or in a career.

Women's Lib? Few women are happy when they are trying to act like a man. Zsa Zsa Gabor said on a talk show, "I want to be more than just equal to a man. I want to be better than a man—and the only way I can do that is to let him think I am less than he is; then he will put me on a pedestal, protect me, and be nice to me—and I will be better off than he is!"

I'm not quite sold on the pedestal but I go for the rest of it. It seems to work out that way.

10

Chamber of Hang-Up Horrors

THEN THERE IS THE PROBLEM of booze and drug addiction. Everywhere I go I hear of young people with hang-ups of one kind or the other.

Some of our sociologists are telling us that it is not dope but alcohol that is the worst of the two problems. (One doctor says it's something else: "Cigarette smoking is, without question, the greatest single health problem this country has ever faced.") I wouldn't know; I'll have to leave it to the sociologists and the doctors and the researchers to determine which is worst. But I haven't any doubt that booze is a bomb that we'd better leave alone.

When I read in *Automotive Engineers' Journal* (July 7, 1970) that alcohol is a factor in at least 800,000 traffic accidents that happen in our country every year, I don't need any expert to tell me that it is a serious problem. The Chicago Traffic Court conducted a study and it was reported in *Presbyterian Outlook* (March 1, 1971) that about half of the nation's highway fatalities were attributed not to hopeless alcoholics but to those who call themselves "only social drinkers". If you think you can "take it or leave it alone," think that one over before you take your first drink. Death on the highway is *quite* social!

I was asked once to make a statement in Texas as to how I felt about voting for the legalizing of liquor-by-the-drink in that state. I declined to do so because, in the first place, I am not a voter in Texas and in the second place I had not come there to engage in a political campaign but to witness for Christ. But I still hold my personal convictions about alcohol—and about drugs and sex and crime—and I believe that their presence indicates a need for the spirit of Christ in frustrated lives. Personally I do not drink, for several reasons. The first reason is that I do not wish to become a stumbling block to someone who is potentially an alcoholic. My Christian witness has been broadcast far and wide for many years, and I do not intend to offend those who are total abstainers. I will not give nonbelievers an opportunity to use my drinking of cocktails as an excuse for their refusal to accept Christ in their lives. I will not offend my brother or sister in either camp. We never know how far our influence will reach, for good or for bad.

I know some Christians who take a cocktail or a glass of wine in clear conscience, and still remain Christians. I also know some wonderfully dedicated

Christians who never touch a drop. Paul wrote in Romans 14:22,23: "Happy is the man who can make his decision with a clear conscience" (The New English Bible). I buy that.

There was a time in my life, before I made my commitment to Christ, when I took a cocktail occasionally because I thought it was something that was expected of me, socially. It never did anything for me except, possibly, to give me a little false courage when I experienced stage fright. The trouble was that one too many always made me sick, and going before the cameras sick just didn't make sense. Once I had the courage of Christ I didn't need the false courage of alcohol. I never had the problem of alcoholism, but my heart aches for those who do have it.

I don't know too much about drugs and narcotics, except that they are fast and deadly. They blast the mind before they murder the body. This idea that they are somehow "spiritual"—that "they lead the user into new and wider spiritual concepts" is blasphemous nonsense. No real leader in any of the world's religions ever advised his followers that they could find God on a wild LSD trip. Psychedelic orgies are *not* spiritual experiences; they are cowardly withdrawals from God and from the problems of human life. When the prophet Joel said that "your old men shall dream dreams, your young men shall see visions" (2:28), he was not referring to the dreams of the

drunken sot or the hallucinations of a drug-crazed mind.

A good friend of mine said to me recently, "The kids don't take dope in rebellion; they take it for kicks."

Maybe so, but it's a pretty stupid way to get kicks. The kicks can knock you flat in your grave—if you can't kick the habit before it gets its grip on you.

Let's take a quick look at some of the things and people who contribute to this drug habit.

Part of the blame rests on the Establishment; I go along with you kids on this. The Establishment is guilty not only of allowing but of actually patronizing a lot of things that encourage youth to seek an escape in pot and heroin. It permits nude movies and dirty books and magazines on the newsstands. You can find topless bars in any city from Boston to L.A.—bars surrounded by dope addicts. The dope pushers hang out there, and the kids are their prey.

We parents are partly to blame. Many fathers and mothers *like* questionable movies, drink too much liquor, even swap partners for the weekend, cheat the government, give (only on Sundays) hypocritical lip service to the Lord; they live on tranquilizers because they can't face up to the tensions and challenges of today's world. How can they expect their children to be better than they are?

When the cop calls them on the phone some terrible

midnight, and says, "We're holding your son on a narcotics charge," they shout, "Oh, no, not my son!"

"Yes, your son."

How inconsistent can we get, as parents? No wonder some kids listen to the pipe dreams of the drug pusher and user. Can't we understand it when you ask, "What's so great about the example set by straight people?" Youth needs honest examples more than they need critics.

I'm not blaming it all on the parents. It isn't all our fault. We all know children who have had all the advantages that good parents can give them, who have had every chance in the world at a good life, and who have still gone on dope; the addicts are not all located on the other side of the tracks but often in our so-called best homes. A lot of it is the fault of youth themselves; they are determined to get their kicks no matter who it hurts. Blaming it all on parents or Establishment, my young friend, is a cheap cop-out.

Cool it, before it burns you alive!

Dope isn't fun; it's fatality. And it takes a lot of fighting faith to cure. In that revival meeting in Texas (which I mentioned previously), a young fellow walked into the office of the First Baptist Church and shook hands with me. At first I wasn't impressed. His hair was too long for my old-fashioned ideas about hair and haircuts. (That doesn't bother me anymore—the twelve disciples had long hair and probably beards, and so did their Master! It isn't the hair that matters; it's the heart!) But there was something in this boy's eyes that fascinated me. There was a strange light in them, and there was a sadness there that said to me, "He's got troubles." As I talked with him, I knew that he was high on Jesus Christ. But....

He came out to the airport to talk more with me the day we left town, and I found out what was behind the sad eyes. This young man was sincerely striving to walk with Christ. He had a hard row to hoe—for too long he had been high on drugs, and the old monkey kept trying to get on his back again; he kept fighting the monkey off. He'd been in the town for only a short time, and he knew few people except the local hippies, and they had been of no help since he was converted to Christ. The temptation to fall back into his old ways was still strong, as he tried so hard to walk Christ's way. He sincerely loved his Lord.

I told him not to be discouraged, not to give up when he stumbled and fell, but to get up and reach out for his Master's Hand; he could be sure the Hand was there—waiting. I told him not to let anyone rob him of his faith in Christ, and to disregard what some well-intentioned but overcritical Christians were saying about his appearance, his hair, and his old habits. I told him to look straight ahead and *up*—not down, nor right, nor left. I told him that the Lord could and would change him into the image He had in mind for him. I thought to myself, "This boy's heart may be cleaner than the hearts of those who condemn him and never lift a finger to help him." "Judge not, that ye be not judged" (Matthew 7:1). I prayed hard that God would steady the light in his eyes—and replace it with the true, steady light which was in Christ.

The plane took off. I left him standing there, so *alone!* Open your eyes and look around, Christian—your world is full of such boys and such struggles. *Help them!* My heart aches for the youth I see standing so alone in the streets and along the highways, thumbing rides to only God knows where. They are searching for peace, reality, love, when all the time it is close and available within themselves, waiting to be tapped!

When I was your age, I was searching, too. We were trapped in the Great Depression; jobs were scarce and the breadlines long, and we struggled to get enough to eat, and to pay the rent. We had our gangs and our hoodlums and our murders and suicides and despairs. But—unlike so many today—we never dreamed of blaming it all on God. We didn't join the hue and cry against Him, nor lump Him together with the evils of capitalism. We realized that our economy was out of balance; but we didn't think it was finished; neither did we yell about abolishing marriage because some people couldn't or wouldn't make it work. And we got through those bad times without proclaiming that God was dead or that the Capitol should be destroyed.

Perhaps, if we get hungry enough again, we will start listening to each other and trying to help each other, and listening to God in a new search together for the Living Water which will satisfy our deepest needs.

We will never conquer the woes of personal and social abuse and injustice through political means, or natural means, or via the escape route. We cannot escape our responsibilities to our fellow men in over-indulgence in dope, alcohol, sex, or wishful thinking. We must, every one of us, understand that "out of the heart proceed evil thoughts, murders, adulteries, fornications, thefts, falsewitness, blasphemies" (Matthew 15:19). We must realize that the human heart is "deceitful above all things, and desperately wicked..." (Jeremiah 17:9). The heart, or the inner person (*your* inner person) must be reborn by the Spirit of the living God. When this takes place, things begin to shape up. Trying to cure the evils that beset us without changing the heart motives that cause it all is like painting an old house that is being eaten to death by termites within. You can pick up a drunk out of the gutter and give him a haircut and a shave and a two-hundred-dollar suit of clothes, but unless you give him a new heart he is still the same old drunk.

God is the answer—God in the heart. If this seems an oversimplification, remember that God is the source of our living. Only in Him, through Jesus Christ, who came that we might have a more abundant life, can the Establishment *and* the NOW generation have a true meeting of the minds.

Yes, Jesus prophesied that the day would come when the children would "rise up against their parents..." (Matthew 10:21). But He also said, "...look up, and lift up your heads; for your redemption draweth nigh" (Luke 21:18).

11

Re-Generation Gap

WE CAN CLOSE the gap if we really *want* to. Let me give you an illustration of what I mean.

A young girl named Judy and I are of two different generations, but there has never been *any* gap between us. I first met her when she was twelve years old, and from the first moment of our acquaintance we could and did communicate; though we were years apart in age, we understood each other then, and we still understand each other. She was something special, good-looking, vivacious, and tremendously alive. She never seemed too young for me to rap with, joyously, on the things that concerned us most. She and I both had a deep, meaningful relationship with the Lord all through her teens and her work as an airline stewardess, into her marriage, and even in the loss of her first-born son. That was the basis of the communication.

Now she is in her thirties, with three beautiful children. She never questioned God about the loss of her first son, and God rewarded her with another, who looked as though he might be the first one returned once again. After him, a darling little girl and another fine little boy. ". . . the Lord gave and the Lord hath taken away; blessed be the name of the Lord" (Job 1:21). Judy believed that, and lived by it. Today she is still very attractive, and definitely "with it" in any crowd. She is a living example of one who early heeded the advice to "Remember now thy Creator in the days of thy youth . . . " (Ecclesiastes 12:1).

Christ was the bridge between us, and still is!

I had another experience with the closing of the gap while Roy and I were appearing at the Arkansas State Fair in Little Rock. I was invited to have breakfast with the Baylor University team on the morning of the day they were to play the University of Arkansas. Tension was high, the excitement terrific; everybody in town was going to the game.

But we had to appear at a rodeo that same night! We were worried about that, with everybody from seven to seventy planning to go to the game. Actually, as it turned out, we had a good crowd, and I was mad at myself for being worried about the competition over there in the stadium—especially when I remembered the respect and close attention the boys gave my witness at the breakfast.

I thanked God for the game. Football rocks with stimulation; it is healthy, invigorating, and constructive. It is great training in teamwork—in fighting for

victory. I've fought all my life for Christian victory,
and for everything else that I have found good, and
I am sick and tired of those in the NOW bunch who
ask for it all to be handed to them on a platter. They
want all the victories without any of the struggles—
and victory just doesn't come that way! Jesus knew
that, so well. He didn't ask for Easter without Good
Friday!

So I thanked God for the football game. It gave
me a chance at the football breakfast to speak for
Him. He closed one door to us that night, and opened
another!

There just isn't any gap, when you see it that way.

A preacher friend down in Texas put what I am
trying to say in twelve beautiful words: "The problem
is not the Generation Gap; it is the *re*-generation gap."
Good! My old friend the dictionary tells me that re-
generation means "To renew spiritually by the power
of the Holy Spirit." That's good, too. The hearts of
young and old, right now, need to be regenerated by
the love and Spirit of Christ, working in and through
them, in their giving and taking, and in exchanging
each other's opinions.

Why do parents fear the opinions of their
children—and vice versa?

This fear of each other's opinions—and actions—
makes me think of the old fellow who stood on the
dock and watched Robert Fulton's first steamboat

getting set for her trip on the Hudson River. He said to his friends, "He'll never get her started." That was old age speaking—old age fearful of such brash youth as Robert Fulton. When the contraption did get started and moved up river against the current, the old fellow said, "Well, he'll never stop her!"

There you have it—fear and power in conflict. In 2 Timothy 1:7, Paul writes to his young friend and assistant, "For God hath not given us the spirit of fear; but of power, and of love, and of a sound mind." Fear? We are all afraid of something or someone. Fear is universal—but it is *not* of God. He did not afflict us with fear of each other, or prejudice toward one another or even fear of Himself. When the Bible speaks of "the fear of God," it means a feeling of awe, wonder, and reverence in the presence of the majesty of God. What God *has* given us is love, and sound minds—and power.

Power? There's a lot of talk about power today, and a lot of it is nonsense. Black power, white power, money power, national power—we sound off about these, but what about the power of God? His power is not built on racial strife or battleships or bombers or money. These powers are negative; His power is positive, bringing a sparkle to the eye, strength in the bones, hope and purpose and confidence in the heart of him who uses the power of God. He has given us the ultimate power of love in the person of His crucified

Son; when we accept that priceless gift of sacrificial love, we grasp the true meaning of life. He infuses us with the Spirit of love and we learn to give that love to others as He gave it to us. Love is not passive, or wistful; it is active, blessing both giver and recipient.

A sound mind? We could use a few more sound minds. Think of the millions spent on psychiatry in this country! And what is psychiatry? It is the study and treatment of mental disease. I've noticed that in too many cases it is a lot stronger on the study than on effective treatment. Psychiatry is able to diagnose, but too often unable to cure *without a measure of faith on the part of the patient*. What kind of power? Faith in a power beyond the psychiatrist and the patient. The psychiatric patient seldom has any real faith in himself; usually that is the primary reason why he goes to the psychiatrist.

If he has no faith in God, in whose image he is made, he's in a pretty bad way!

When we think of the word *sound*, we think of *solid*—whole, complete, dependable, not erratic, but *sure*. Today, it's considered square to be sure of anything. With this kind of thinking, the only thing you can be certain about is your uncertainty, and where does that leave you? It leaves you like a squirrel on a treadmill running furiously and getting nowhere. What's so free about that? Is frustration in uncertainty *freedom?*

It reminds me of the child whose father builds a house of blocks for him to play with. The child has so many toys around him that he doesn't appreciate any of them—and probably doesn't appreciate his father, either. So he knocks down the house of blocks with a sweep of his hand. Then he tries to rebuild it "like I want it." And he can't. He hasn't any blueprints.

Youth, show us your blueprints! If you are so uncertain about the old house we have given you to live in, take a tip from me: Don't knock it down unless and until you have the plans drawn for another one. Destroy the institutions and the establishments we have built, and what do you have left upon which to build something better? (But I do not doubt that you *can* build something better.)

I agree with Dr. Arthur H. Cain, who writes: "If there is still anyone anywhere today who would like for things to remain exactly as they have been in the United States for the past fifty years, then I would have to say that he is my enemy." But if you don't mind, I'd like to see your blueprints for the future, because I have to live in that future, too. This is my country, as well as yours.

Let's say you destroy the educational system that so many of you say is in such a horrible condition. What kind of schools do you propose for tomorrow? Exactly what and how do you propose to rebuild? On rock 'n' roll, flowers, dope, and sex? You know better.

You will be asking for our tax money to build it.
Would that be taxation without representation—and
do you want that? You paint a very rosy picture of
the lackadaisical, slaphappy, rocking, and rolling com-
munity for tomorrow—but who is going to plant the
crops and reap the wheat and man the factories and
distribute the goods and sign your welfare checks?

Who's kidding who, about all this?

12

Interviewing the Interviewer

NOT LONG AGO I was interviewed by a very intense and mod young woman who let me know (before we even got started) that she didn't think very much of my ideas (she hadn't heard them from me, yet) or of the old Victorian values that most of us liked and lived by. She thought that both the values and I were hopelessly irrelevant and passé. As an interviewer, she had her points, and they were all sharp. She was as much entitled to her own opinions as I was, so I let her run on and waited for her first question. She asked: "What do you think about the youth revolution, the demonstrations in the streets, and on the campus?"

"This country," I replied, "was founded on the teachings and tenets of the Bible; if you have read the Mayflower Compact and other statements of the early colonists who came here seeking not just economic opportunity but religious freedom even more, you know about that." (From her reaction I wasn't sure she knew about that, but ... !) "It was founded by people who believed in God, in His Word, in Jesus

Christ, in the Holy Spirit working out His purposes in humanity. In a long and painful development they worked out a way of life and government on a guarantee of freedom that is, today, the envy of every people on the face of the earth. Not very many are leaving the United States, but you can find people everywhere in the world who want to come here. Would you call that bad, or good? The fact that some people abuse this freedom under God and even use it to destroy it doesn't make the basis of that freedom irrelevant, does it?"

She didn't answer that. She started to ask another quite different question, but I pushed the point a little further. "In what country, where God is denied, can you get away with burning the flag, condemning the government, advocating a nationwide murder of policemen?" No answer.

I made the flat statement that Jesus Christ is completely contemporary and relevant for today. She almost screamed, "For instance?" I replied, "The Bible tells us that God is love—and love is hardly irrelevant in any generation; even the hippies and the most radical leftists on the current scene keep talking about 'love—love,' and it is difficult for some of us to reconcile this love with the fire bombs they hide behind their backs. 'Love, not war!' Is that new? Jesus Christ preached it and died for it. He was the personification of love at its best—Godlike, sacrificial.

His greatest crime, in the eyes of His enemies, was that He even loved publicans and sinners. Would you call that irrelevant? The few moments when He was really angry with anybody were moments triggered by people like the moneychangers who were cheating the people in the shadow of the Temple, and at the Pharisees who were piously hypocritical and judgmental with a spirit-hungry people who should have been given bread instead of pharisaical stones."

The word *hypocritical* got under her skin. When I went a step further and said that Jesus relates directly to the disdain of the campus and street protestors, she broke in with a command: "Explain that!"

I reminded her of the story of the woman taken in adultery, and of His challenge to the men who were about to stone her. " ... He that is without sin among you, let him first cast a stone at her" (John 8:7). He was telling them to examine their own sinful characters before they accused another of a sin that was quite familiar to them, in their own lives. I mentioned His condemnation of men who polished the outside of the cup and left the inside foul and unclean. "Ye hypocrites ..." (Matthew 15:7)!

"But," she asked, "what does all that have to do with hypocrisy today?"

I asked her if there were ever times in her life when she felt like a hypocrite—was she always satisfied with her behavior, with what she was, and wasn't? She was honest enough to answer, "No, I'm not." I asked her if she had ever claimed freedom from a bad habit and denounced others who were possessed by it, and then in a weak moment fell flat on her face and indulged in the habit all over again. She said slowly, "I see what you mean." As gently as I could, I pointed out that we all fall short of the glory of God, of His high potential for our lives, and even fall short of the standards we set for ourselves. Did she ever feel like that? Yes, she did.

I asked her about her idea of God. (Let me give you a tip—when you meet up with an unsympathetic, antagonistic interviewer, don't let him ask all the questions. Throw some at him. Put *him* on the defensive!) Did she think of God as an old man with a whip, just waiting for her to make a mistake? If she did, she'd better get herself another God. I quoted Jesus. "God is a Spirit [a loving Spirit!]: and they that worship him must worship him in spirit and in truth" (John 4:24). I told her that I believed that the true and ultimate inspiration for right action was the Spirit of God breaking through in the human mind and heart. Had she ever encouraged that breaking through? Had she ever really thought through these words of Jesus Christ, ever invited Him into her heart? I asked her point-blank if she considered herself a Christian.

She said she hadn't made up her mind about that,

or about who or what God was. She felt that people could set their own ideals and standards and love their fellow men without God in the picture at all. To me, that was impossible; it hadn't worked out that way in my experience, and I couldn't believe that it would work out in hers, and I told her so. I asked her to read my testimony in *The Woman at the Well*, objectively, and she promised to do so. I had to settle for that, and we went our separate ways.

She gave me a rough ride. Her heckling style reminded me of the heckling of Jesus by the Pharisees and I had to struggle, as He did, to be calm and cool and reasonable toward her for I loved her, and she was important to God. He paid a great price for her on Calvary; He offered her a freedom and a life that passed all understanding, and a passport to eternal life. It can still be hers, if she wants it.

I pray for her.

13

A Goal for Both Generations

LET ME SAY AGAIN: *I do not hold with the defeatists who say that all is lost with our youth.* I am constantly amazed at their dedication and spiritual insights.

Our daughter-in-law, Linda, wrote me at Christmas time.

We give thanks that we are as fortunate as we are. I feel ashamed when I surrender to feeling sorry for myself and start complaining about what seems to be some important problem, and then I think of the greater problem of people all over the world who are starving, clothesless, homeless—and never expecting a Christmas. Oh, we do give some small contributions which do help, but what a wonderful Christmas it would be if we would *all* help the needy! I only hope our children will grow up thankful and appreciative for what they have and not like so many of us who want more, more, more .... I guess I can't put all the blame on our generation, though; we've never known poverty and depression, only good times. And you really can't blame the parents who wanted something more for their children than they had themselves. Let's pray that the new generation will do something constructive for this world before we destroy it beyond repair.

Linda is in her twenties; she typifies so many of you, the NOW generation which, I believe, perceives more than the Establishment realizes. You're searching, and I'm for you in your search.

A friend has just sent me a startling little book—*Christ Is Alive*, by Michel Quoist. Last night I read:

We firmly believe that modern man and the modern world, without being conscious of it, are calling to God with all their strength. That call is often a silent one, from the subconscious of individuals or from that of mankind collectively. But sometimes it is the desperate cry of men victimized and crushed by our great "consumer society" of men who are supposed to be the beneficiaries, but become the slaves of that society. That cry comes principally from the young who, before they can be anesthetized and smothered by the urge to "have" scream out their hunger to "be." Often, they have no idea of what it is they want to be or of what they should be. Their rebellion is a revolt, which takes place in the most complete disorder, against everything that appears to limit man in his body, his mind, his love, and in the desire to surpass himself by attaining a degree of development and expansion as yet undreamed of. . . . Thus, these young people demand, and often live, sexual freedom. They are looking for a love to satisfy their famished bodies, but without taking into account that their hunger comes from beyond the body. It is a hunger of the soul, and it rises above the body through which it is felt. Thus, they attempt to penetrate into "another world" by means of drugs and esoteric cults; or they simply try to establish a new life-style by cultivating "originality" and experimenting in human relationships—hence the phenomena of the hippies, the beatniks, and so forth. All of this, very likely, is founded in discouragement and disillusionment with realistic efforts to build a new society; but it also reflects a will to question values deeply at a time when, in the face of so many failures, the desire and the vision of a beautiful future is growing.

This, to me, is a fine realistic approach to this pressing problem of our times. But may I be bold enough to add to it my conviction that it isn't a problem unique to the younger generation! It may have a greater urgency now than it had in the past, but there has always been questioning and revolt and a passion for something better. Yet in spite of all the questioning and quarreling, God's truth has been marching on, and I think our effort today, in both generations, should be to join that march.

What is this truth? Truth is Jesus Christ, His Sonship with God, His effective, redemptive, remedial sacrifice on the Cross for the sins of the world. His Resurrection and the Resurrection through the Spirit of those who believe and accept the Truth of His being and through it enter into new life.

That may be hard to swallow, for it involves the swallowing of our human pride—the pride that caused the downfall of man in the first place—men wanting to be equal with their Creator. Pride is a tyrant; humility brings peace and the only freedom worth having.

Proud tyrants crucified Him. They couldn't stand His humility. But if our world is to be saved at all it will be saved by the practice of that sacrificial humility, and in no other way.

14

Drop In, Not Out

THERE'S A LOT of rapping about the church today, particularly among the younger NOWS. You hear a lot of them saying that the church is dead or dying, and besides, "I've got my own religion; who needs the church?" They're fed up with so-called organized religion. That's for old folks who want to warm themselves, not for the lively young ones. And the older ones are bemoaning the exodus of the young from the church.

Too many of them are leaving—no doubt about that. But where do they go, once they leave it? Some are going into what they call the Underground Church, which, if they look at it carefully, is becoming something of an organization itself. Others are turning to astrology, horoscopes, ESP, spiritism, Ouija boards, crystal ball, or Zen Buddhism. I feel sorry for them, for I believe that in turning from organized Christianity to the gadgetry of the sects they are still a religious generation seeking some rock to cling to for security in a world gone mad!

I think, too, that many of them leave what they *think* is the church without having thought their way through to a concept of the church that is really good and honest and intelligent. They talk as though all of the churches are the same—just one big family with one common, conventional form of religious faith and activity. That's nonsense! It's like saying that all the books in your public library are the same. You can find anything in the church from Unitarianism to Two-Seed-in-the-Spirit-Predestinarian Baptists. There is room in the church for all of us, and it is a poor cop-out to say that you are leaving the churches because "they are all the same." You can pick and choose—but be careful! Don't just pick any old church; find out, before you join, if you are going to get what you hunger for in the one you join.

Organized? Of course the church is organized. What isn't today? Was the school you attended organized? Is the store where you buy your food organized? Are our rioting students organized? Some of those on welfare are anti-Establishment; but they don't object to taking their welfare checks from an organized welfare program. Why should they object to an organization created to help meet their spiritual needs?

Any movement requires organization, but all organizations are not the same. The church is one made up of human beings—which accounts for a lot of its shortcomings!—and of believers in Jesus Christ who admit that they fall far short of His model but who at least are trying to follow Him, and who need the sympathy and help of the church.

The denomination is a fellowship. Someone has to shepherd that fellowship, and so we have to pay our full-time ministers (who may be the most underpaid group of professionals in the country). If you have an assembly of people, you must have some place for them to assemble; you must have a building for them, and that building has to be maintained. Our Bible study materials cost money to print—they must be purchased. Jesus commanded us to send the gospel to every creature, and so we send missionaries abroad, and missionaries have to eat, too. Have you ever stopped to figure out what it costs to support the church-related hospitals and the homes for children and the aged, in the United States? Yes, it's an organization; can you name one that does more to help humanity?

I think sometimes that a lot of these people who oppose the church and drop out of it do so because they don't want to contribute to it. That's odd. They will pay a doctor for treating their physical ills, but balk at supporting a hospital dedicated to the treatment of their spiritual ills! They are quite willing to accept the good fruits of the churches in its thinkers, artists, charitable works, and workers, but they reject any demand on their time, energy, or pocketbooks.

They want all that—*gratis*. The next time you hear an exchurchman say that the church is dead, ask him how much he contributed last year to keep it alive.

Why are so many young rebels fed up with the church? Let's be honest, here. One good reason is that the church, too often, has not met their needs. Some churches argue about a lot of questions that youth never asks, and offered feeble answers to a lot of questions they do ask.

In the field of morality, for instance, many a church has pussyfooted and dodged and been afraid to take a Christian stand on moral problems. Immorality is still immorality, no matter how you try to sugarcoat it. Young people have no respect for Christians who try to excuse their immoral behavior by trying to read permissive premarital sex into the Scripture, when the Bible lays down very plain and simple ground rules about it. Or they excuse their drinking on the ground that "Jesus made wine at Cana"! There is a price to be paid for the breaking of God's law within or without the church. They should understand that God is completely faithful and just and that He recompenses us for every deed, good or bad. He is not mocked. What we sow, we reap. Sometimes the payment is deferred, but we pay, whether we are church members or anti-church.

Some young people are leaving the church because of the hypocrisy they observe in the churchmen. We

in the church plead guilty; we do have a lot of hypocrites hanging around—but do we have more than our
share of them? You can find hypocrites among the
lawyers and the doctors and the businessmen and
even among the atheists. The church has no corner on
hypocrisy. When a young man told Dwight L. Moody
that he couldn't join a church because it was full of
hypocrites, Moody replied, "You're right. We have
some hypocrites. But come on in—there's always
room for one more."

We parents, we older Christians, can correct this
sad situation by showing that in our own lives Christ
has been sufficient for our problems. When youth sees
the parents meeting a crucial test with Christian faith
and confidence, they will be impressed and not dis-
gusted. They will not stay in the church simply because we tell them to—they want a better reason than
that, and if our lives are right with Christ, they will
have that reason.

The church isn't a social club; it is a combination
school-and-hospital for the soul.

Dr. David H. C. Read, in a little book entitled *Over-
heard*, sums it up beautifully when he says:

If I were bold enough . . . what I should really like
to say when I overhear the remark, "I've got my
own religion; who needs a church?" is "You
borrowed your religion [from the church] and

you're paying nothing back; and you *do* need a church because none of us can ultimately go it alone, because the church is the carrier of the faith from one generation to another, because we all need the strength and discipline she offers, because the church needs you."

Think twice, youth, before you drop out!

In my mother's church bulletin, the pastor wrote this:

It is tremendously important that we are always conscious of the fact that every day we are sowing seed which will take root and grow, and grow, and grow, until it is fully grown, and the harvest time is upon us. Every day we are sowing either the flesh or the Spirit, whether we are aware of it or not. It is absolutely certain that we will reap what we have sown! It is also certain that we will reap an abundant harvest. You sow one grain of corn; but you reap many grains from the ears of corn that one grain produces. So it is with our lives, which we are living every day. Be sure (very sure) your sin will find you out.

The seeds of faith, sown early in the child by the parents, produce abundance, one way or the other.

Some folks don't seem to understand or believe this. I have just received a letter from a woman who complains that my books, *Time Out, Ladies,* and *The Woman at the Well,* have upset her neat little package of unbelief. She says that she "had religion shoved, jammed, and stuffed down her throat until, unable to stand it any longer, I threw it back at them, and renounced my baptismal and confirmation vows." This is not the first time I have heard that one—nor will it be the last. Long before I even thought of being used by the Lord to witness by writing—when I was far from giving Him any place in my life's direction—I heard them say the same thing: "Once I am far away from home and parents, I doubt that I will ever go to church again."

Let's break down that complaint, and examine it. We all have to be taught when we are young. God has commissioned the parent to "train up a child in the way he should go," and the parent who says, "I am not going to suggest anything about religion to my child; he can choose his own way," would not dream of letting a toddler run out into the traffic of the street by himself. Nor would he give the toddler the key to the family medicine chest. Nor would he refuse to send the child to school if he didn't want to learn, and allow him just to stay at home and do his own thing.

Nonsense! We have a parental obligation *to nurture the whole person in the child*, not just his body, but his mind and his soul as well. Even if we know our children may throw off the yoke as soon as they leave the nest of home, we must at least expose them to what God has revealed for mankind's good. We do not have to coerce them into joining the church early in their lives, but certainly they should learn early of God, Christ, and the Bible, for the Bible contains an account of the spiritual history of man, the finest philosophy by which he can live, and—most important of all—the keys to salvation and eternal life. That seed must be sown.

The plain truth is that the flesh will always be in conflict with the Spirit. The flesh does not want to be denied anything, even harmful things. But "It is the spirit that quickeneth; the flesh profiteth nothing . . ." (John 6:63). Yes, it's the Spirit that brings life to the person.

So why not nourish the Spirit?

No matter how complex our problems, how fraught with evil, the living, glorious Christ still says to you, "Come unto me, all ye that labour and are heavy laden, and I will give you rest" (Matthew 11:28). He can give you more. He can give the heart wings of joy. He can impart shining hope, a willingness to bear one another's burdens, and love for one another. He sends His Holy Spirit to guide us into all truth. He never promised that the way would be easy, but He promised a safe and sure path through the wilderness. "From whence comes our help?" "Our help is in the name of the Lord, who made heaven and earth" (Psalms 124:8).

You young people of the NOW, reach out and find and stand with Him in new responsibility to Him and to your fellow man. It may just be that we of the Establishment have had our day; at least, the future belongs to you. But please remember this, from a veteran who has been over the road before you, you will destroy all hope in the future unless you face it in the company of Jesus Christ. You will not fail, if He is with you, for there is a light within you placed there by His very hand.

Until you turn on the switch of faith and then feed that inner need within, you will continue to grapple in darkness. Reach for the switch! Lead your generation responsibly, and plant deep the seeds of faith and truth to guide the generation that will come after yours.

We do not know when the Lord shall return. There are seemingly good signs that this Great Day is not far distant, but until that Day comes, let us all lift up our heads—not in doubt—but in faith, square our stooping shoulders, clasp hands, and walk forward and upward together.

And, as Roy would say, "May the good Lord take a liking to you."